LEADGEN UNLEASHED

100 WAYS TO CLIENT ATTRACTION

100 Proven lead gen strategies for smal businesses & entrepreneurs who want to build a client attraction system.

JESSICA **CAMPOS**

Copyright © 2023 by Jessica Campos

All rights reserved.

ISBN: 9798858010517

Table of Contents

Special Words of Appreciation 5

Introduction 7

1. Understanding the Landscape of Lead Generation 11

2. Building a Client Attraction System 33

    6 Key Components of a Successful Client Attraction System 36

    1. Defining Your Target Audience 36

    2. Value Proposition 37

    3. Touchpoints 41

    4. Irresistible Offer 49

    5. Personalization 51

    6. Lead Nurturing 55

3. 100 Ways to Generate Leads 59

    Social Media (1-20) 59

    Content Marketing (21-40) 61

    Guerilla Marketing (41-50) 63

    Demand Generation Campaigns (51-75) 64

    Co-Marketing (76-85) 67

    Leveraging Platforms (86-100) 68

4. Overcoming Lead Generation Roadblocks 73

5. Unlocking Growth with Forensic Marketing...............77
   Key Forensic Marketing Tools......................................78

6. AI Marketing - The Cutting Edge of Lead Generation 81
   The 50-50 AI Marketing Framework...........................83
   Best Uses of AI Marketing for Business Owners..........85

7. The Mindset for Rapid Business Growth....................91

   About Jessica Campos, Founder of Marketing for Greatness..95

Special Words of Appreciation

First and foremost, I want to extend my heartfelt gratitude to my team. Each of you has played a vital role in not only the success of our business but also in bringing this book to life. Your dedication, creativity, and unwavering support have been nothing short of inspiring.

To my business partners Alex and Carolina, thank you for embarking on this incredible journey with me. Your vision, expertise, and relentless drive have been the backbone of our success. Together, we've turned dreams into reality, and I am profoundly grateful for our collaboration.

To my dear friend Albania, affectionately known as Dr. Alby, your influence and support have been a beacon of light in this part of my journey. Your wisdom, encouragement, and genuine friendship have meant more to me than words can express. Thank you for being an incredible piece of this adventure. Your presence in my life has been a true blessing.

To Julia, the Content Hacker and Queen, your guidance and mentorship have illuminated the roadmap to the world of content, enabling me to navigate with confidence and skill. Your passion, expertise, and unwavering support have not only enriched my understanding but have sparked a collaboration that I cherish. I'm filled with anticipation and excitement for what the future holds for us, and I thank you profoundly for being a vital part of my journey!

Lastly, but by no means least, my deepest thanks go to my family. Your love, encouragement, and belief in me have been my guiding light. You've stood by me through the ups and downs, always offering a word of encouragement or a listening ear. I could not have achieved this without you.

This book is a testament to what can be achieved when you surround yourself with people who believe in you and your vision. Thank you all, from the bottom of my heart. Your faith in me has made all the difference.

Introduction

Imagine you're John, a seasoned sales professional who has just landed a coveted position at a thriving tech firm. Throughout your career, you've transformed innovative sales strategies into significant revenue, all thanks to your secret weapon: Lead generation.

Now, imagine you're Sarah, a small business owner who has launched a successful online store selling handmade jewelry. You started your business from a place of passion and creativity, but you soon realized that to grow your business, you needed to understand and master lead generation.

Perhaps you see yourself in John, Sarah, or a combination of both. As professionals seeking to monetize your content, aren't you also looking to create an influx of potential clients? Don't you want to cultivate real connections, meaningful conversations that open up a world of possibilities?

To turn these interactions into tailored advice that addresses the unique needs of your audience, leading them to ask, "Could you help us with that?"

John's and Sarah's stories might be fictional, yet they mirror many of your experiences. You, like them, are on a mission to enhance your sales, to navigate the complex labyrinth of lead generation. And that's why you're here.

Welcome to "100 Ways to Generate Leads: Build Your Client Attraction System Today!" This guide dives deep into the realm of lead generation, equipping you with the knowledge and tools you need to build a robust lead generation system.

Whether you're a sales pro like John, a small business owner like Sarah, a savvy consultant, or an ambitious entrepreneur, this guide is for you. It doesn't matter if you're a beginner who is just starting your journey or an experienced professional looking to refine your skills; this book will help you generate leads and achieve your goals.

We all know that for entrepreneurs or small business owners, lead generation is the lifeblood of your operations. It's the difference between a thriving business and one that barely survives. But without a clear roadmap, the competitive landscape can feel overwhelming, even insurmountable. This e-book is your compass, guiding you to uncover what makes your potential clients tick and helping you outperform your competition.

Inside, you'll find 100 proven strategies, all designed to help you master the art of lead generation. These aren't just theories; they are practical, actionable methods that have been tested and honed over time. Each one has played a significant role in generating multiple 7-figure revenues for businesses across various industries. They represent the pinnacle of lead generation strategies, the culmination of years of research, experimentation, and learning from the best in the business.

But the journey doesn't stop here. Alongside this e-book, I also offer a unique program called "88 To Great," a selection of done-for-you and done-with-you services for business owners and marketing teams ready to turbocharge their lead generation efforts.

Our "88 To Great" program is designed to provide hands-on, personalized support as you implement the strategies outlined in this book.

The done-for-you service within the "88 To Great" program is perfect for professionals who prefer to focus on their core business activities while letting a team of experts handle their lead generation efforts. We'll take the reins, applying our proven strategies to attract and engage your ideal clients, saving you time and ensuring you can maintain your focus where it's needed most.

Alternatively, the done-with-you service within "88 To Great" is ideal for those who prefer a more collaborative approach. We'll work side-by-side with you, teaching you the ins and outs of effective lead generation, and helping you to implement these strategies in your business. This approach not only provides immediate results but also equips you with the skills and knowledge to continue generating leads long after our work together is done.

Both services within "88 To Great" are tailored to your unique needs, ensuring you receive the support that best aligns with your business goals and working style. So, whether you're looking to delegate your lead generation efforts entirely or wishing to learn from experts while actively participating in the process, "88 To Great" has you covered.

Now, are you ready to step into John's or Sarah's shoes and embark on this transformative journey? Are you prepared to take your business to the next level? Let's dive in and start building your client attraction system today. Together, with the "88 To Great" program, we can turn your passion into revenue, your ideas into action, and your potential leads into loyal customers.

Chapter 1

Understanding the Landscape of Lead Generation

'Lead' is a term that can vary in meaning depending on the industry context. It can often be intertwined with terms like suspects, prospects, qualified marketing leads, and qualified sales leads, leading to confusion. So, let's clarify what leads truly represent in the business landscape.

Understanding the Concept of a Leads

In simple terms, a lead is a potential customer with an interest in your product or service. However, the process of converting this potential customer into an actual one is entirely up to you. It's essential to understand that not all lead categories carry the same value. Understanding the various types of leads is crucial for effective lead management. (Don't worry, this won't take much time).

Differentiating Between a Lead and a Prospect

A lead, as we've established, is a potential customer with an interest in a product or service. A prospect, on the other hand, is a potential customer with a heightened level of interest, making them more likely to convert (or make a purchase).

This distinction, although subtle, has a substantial impact on business operations. To simplify, a prospect is a qualified lead; you've already invested resources in assessing their interest. Therefore, the process of converting them into sales is considerably less complex.

Consider the example of an online clothing store. A lead could be someone subscribed to your email list for promotional updates and may make a purchase in the future. In contrast, a prospect is one step ahead; they have items in their cart or have consistently browsed a specific product.

Understanding these differences is vital as it allows you to target your marketing efforts more accurately. Tailoring your approach to each group's level of engagement can significantly improve conversion rates. For instance, you can entice prospects with targeted ads or exclusive discounts, incentivizing them to complete their purchase.

To summarize, leads are at the beginning of the sales funnel, while prospects are further along and have engaged with your brand in a more significant manner.

Distinguishing Between a Prospect and a Suspect

Depending on your industry, you might have heard about suspects and prospects. Prospects are relatively lower in the sales funnel with a higher business interest, while suspects are in the initial stages and may not be ready for conversion yet.

Suspects interact with your brand in various ways, such as visiting your website, following you on social media, or subscribing to your email list. However, they haven't shown a clear intention of becoming a paying customer yet.

As suspects are potential leads, marketing teams focus on generating suspects through various channels. The more a suspect shows interest in the business, the higher they move within the sales funnel. Once they surpass a certain engagement level, they are handed over to the sales team for follow-up.

Characteristics of a Prospect and a Suspect

Prospects generally share certain characteristics:

- They have a specific problem or need that your product or service can solve.

- They have engaged with your brand through various marketing channels.

- They have shown interest in your product or service.

- They fit the profile of your target audience based on their demographics, behavior, or interests.

Suspects, on the other hand, differ in the following ways:

- They may have come across your brand but do not necessarily have a specific need for your product or service.

- They have not engaged with your brand in any significant way.

- They may not fit the profile of your target audience.

What About Your Instagram Followers?

If you're like most of our clients, you're looking to grow your audience on Instagram with the ultimate goal of increasing your revenue. A larger following can indeed open up opportunities for business growth, but it's essential to understand that not all followers are created equal. For effective marketing and sales strategies, it's crucial to differentiate between 'prospects' and 'suspects' within your follower base.

Prospects vs. Suspects

Suspects are followers who have shown a basic level of interest by following your account. However, their interaction might not extend beyond that initial follow. They haven't significantly engaged with your posts and haven't shown clear signs of interest in your offerings. They are individuals you suspect might be interested in what you have to offer, but there's no substantial evidence to confirm this yet.

In contrast, **prospects** are followers who have displayed a higher level of interest in your products or services. They frequently engage with your posts, visit your website, sign up for your newsletters, download your content, or may have even reached out directly for more information. These are the followers who are more likely to transition from just being interested to becoming actual customers.

Leveraging Content Marketing to Identify and Nurture Prospects

One effective way to differentiate between suspects and prospects, and to guide them towards becoming customers, is to create a content marketing funnel on Instagram. This strategy involves producing and sharing content that attracts, engages, and ultimately converts your followers:

1. **Awareness Stage:** At this stage, you aim to reach a broad audience and create awareness about your brand. This can be achieved through blog posts, infographics, videos, and engaging social media posts related to popular topics in your industry.

2. **Interest Stage:** Once you've grabbed their attention, engage your suspects with more in-depth content that adds real value. This could be through sharing how-to guides, case studies, webinars, or eBooks to demonstrate how your product or service can solve their problems or enhance their lives.

3. **Consideration Stage:** At this point, your prospects are seriously considering making a purchase. Nurture this interest with content like product demonstrations, customer testimonials, and detailed comparison guides. Offering free trials or consultations could also be beneficial.

4. **Conversion Stage:** After nurturing your prospects, the final step is to convert them into customers. Make the purchasing process as straightforward as possible, offering various payment options, and provide excellent customer service.

In the realm of social media marketing, the primary goal isn't merely to drive leads and sales. It's about cultivating a meaningful relationship with your followers, guiding them through a journey from being 'suspects' to 'prospects', and eventually, to becoming loyal customers. This evolution represents a shift in their engagement and interest in your brand, and understanding this can help you design more effective marketing strategies.

Leads Are Humans, Not Numbers

Before we delve into the tactics, it's crucial to lay down some ground rules to set the right expectations. The strategies I'm going to share will assist you in generating leads. However, it's important to remember that leads are not equivalent to sales. More significantly, leads are humans, not mere numbers in your spreadsheet.

Why this warning? Because the digital marketing world is teeming with templates promoting immediate purchases with "buy now" buttons. This approach tends to treat leads merely as potential sales, often overlooking the human aspect of the equation.

Let's take a moment to incorporate some insights from both neuromarketing and the psychology of online purchases.

Before you can generate leads, you need visibility. Visibility means that your ideal buyers are seeing your offers. These buyers will embark on a journey to decide whether to purchase from you or hire your services. But, will they buy from you in one click? Probably not.

Inbound marketing stats show that 47% of buyers view 3-5 pieces of content before engaging with a sales rep. This reveals an important aspect of the online purchasing journey – it's a process that involves research, consideration, and comparison.

1. **Emotions are powerful drivers**: A study by the Harvard Business Review found that emotionally engaged customers are at least three times more likely to recommend a product and repurchase it. So, creating a connection that elicits positive emotions can be a powerful lead conversion tool.

2. **The power of storytelling**: Our brains are wired to respond to stories. A study published in the Annual Review of Psychology showed that narratives engage more parts of our brain than facts alone. This makes storytelling a potent tool in marketing.

3. **The Principle of Reciprocity**: Neuromarketing studies have revealed that humans have an inherent desire to

return favors. This principle can be used in lead generation by offering value (like a free e-book or a discount code) to potential leads, increasing the likelihood of them making a purchase in return.

4. **Scarcity and Urgency**: The brain is naturally drawn to things that are rare or time-limited. Marketers can leverage this by creating urgency or scarcity in their campaigns (limited time offers, limited stock, etc.), which can prompt leads to act.

The psychology of online purchasing also reveals that trust is a significant factor influencing online purchases. A survey by BrightLocal found that 84% of people trust online reviews as much as personal recommendations, and 91% of people read online reviews to determine the quality of a local business.

So, it's crucial to build credibility and trust with your leads through testimonials, reviews, and high-quality, informative content.

Remember, while these neuromarketing strategies can enhance your lead generation, it's crucial to respect the fact that leads are humans with their own unique needs, desires, and decision-making processes. By acknowledging and catering to this human element, your lead generation tactics will be more effective, resulting in not just more leads, but leads that are more likely to convert into sales.

The Human Connection in Lead Generation

You're reading this right. We might be able to ignite your leads online, but you might need to talk to humans!

Why am I emphasizing this?

Let me share a story about a client we'll call Tracy - to maintain anonymity, of course. Tracy approached my SEO agency with a mission: she wanted to generate a massive amount of traffic for her website. Now, Tracy's website was adorned with shiny "buy now" buttons, which you might expect for an e-commerce site. But here's the twist: Tracy was a coach, trying to sell coaching packages.

Seeing those "buy now" buttons, I suggested to Tracy we might want to consider replacing them with a call to action that offers a free consultation. In my experience, that's a much more effective way to approach prospective coaching clients, providing a taste of the value they'd get before they commit.

However, Tracy's response was unexpected. She flatly refused, saying, "No, I don't want to talk to people". This was surprising. As a coach, building relationships is crucial. Engaging in one-on-one interactions, providing value, and understanding your clients' needs are often the keys to converting prospects into paying customers.

So we had a unique challenge. A coach who didn't want to personally connect with potential clients but wanted to increase her client base.

The internet is a wild place, full of less than stellar advice. It's got folks believing that they can just slap up a website, kick back, and watch the dollars roll in as they sleep. But let's be real here: it just doesn't work like that.

Tracy ultimately reassessed and came to a crucial understanding. She recognized the golden rule: people do business with people. They want to know who's behind the business, who they're trusting, and who they're investing their hard-earned money with. They crave that personal touch, that human connection.

So what did Tracy do? She decided to hire a virtual assistant to handle her conversations. A smart move on her part. By doing so, she created a bridge of communication between her business and her prospective clients. Even though Tracy might not be the one directly interacting, her VA ensured that the human connection wasn't lost. And that's a win in my book!

If you're hoping for some magical artificial intelligence to take the reins, turn your business into a money-making machine while you sleep, this strategy might not be your cup of tea.

However, if you believe that your business has the potential to create a real impact, to make a genuine difference in people's lives, then keep reading. This strategy is for those who are all about providing the kind of customer service that people can't stop raving about. It's for those who aspire to build a brand that they're immensely proud to stand behind.

Most importantly, it's for those who understand that a lead isn't just a statistic. It's not a cold, hard number on a screen. A lead is a person. A human being with wants, needs, and desires that your business has the potential to fulfill.

Don't get me wrong, though. This doesn't mean we're going to ignore the numbers. Far from it! We're going to dive deep into how you can effectively quantify leads, measure transactions, and accurately track your revenue. But let's never forget that behind each of those numbers, there's a human story.

Boosting Revenue: The Dual Power of Visibility and Conversions

In the competitive landscape of business, increasing revenue is a common goal shared by all. However, achieving this requires a strategic approach and a deep understanding of two critical areas: visibility and conversion. If you want to grow your revenue, you need to either increase your visibility or improve your conversions, and often, businesses are lacking in visibility.

The Power of Visibility

Visibility refers to how visible your business is to potential customers. It involves making your business known and putting your products and services in front of potential customers. This can be achieved through various marketing and advertising strategies, from traditional methods like print advertising and direct mail to digital methods like search engine optimization, social media marketing, and content marketing.

Most businesses struggle with visibility. They may have a great product or offer an exceptional service, but if people aren't aware of it, they can't become customers. Therefore, increasing your visibility is often the first step towards growing your revenue.

Here are some strategies to increase your business visibility:

1. **SEO (Search Engine Optimization):** This involves optimizing your website and online content to rank higher on search engine results pages. This can lead to increased traffic to your website and more potential customers discovering your business.

2. **Content Marketing:** Creating valuable and engaging content can attract potential customers to your business. This could be through blogging, creating videos, hosting webinars, or developing a podcast.

3. **Social Media Marketing:** Utilizing social media platforms can help you reach a wider audience. Regularly posting engaging content and interacting with your audience can increase your visibility and brand awareness.

4. **Paid Advertising:** This includes strategies like pay-per-click advertising, social media ads, and sponsored content. Paid advertising can give your visibility a significant boost.

The Power of Conversion

While visibility is about attracting potential customers, conversion is about turning those potential customers into actual customers. Increasing your conversion rate is just as important as increasing visibility when it comes to growing your revenue.

Here are some strategies to improve your conversion rate:

1. **Website Optimization:** Make sure your website is user-friendly, easy to navigate, and clearly communicates your value proposition. A well-designed website can significantly improve your conversion rate.

2. **A/B Testing:** This involves testing different versions of your website or marketing materials to see which one performs better. This can help you identify what resonates most with your audience and optimize accordingly.

3. **Customer Journey Mapping:** Understanding your customer's journey can help you identify any barriers or pain points that might be preventing them from converting. You can then address these issues to improve your conversion rate.

4. **Personalization:** Personalizing your marketing messages and website experience can make potential customers feel more valued and understood, which can increase your conversion rate.

In conclusion, if you want to grow your revenue, you need to focus on both increasing your visibility and improving your conversions. These two areas work hand in hand - you need visibility to attract potential customers, and you need conversions to turn those potential customers into actual revenue.

Marketing Leads vs. Sales Leads

An important distinction in lead generation is understanding the difference between marketing leads and sales leads.

Marketing leads are contacts who have shown some initial interest in your business by downloading content or signing up for something on your website. But they haven't necessarily committed to making a purchase yet.

Sales leads are contacts who are further down the funnel and have indicated stronger buying intent. For example, requesting a demo, signing up for a free trial, or inquiring about pricing.

While marketing leads are great for building your audience and subscribers, sales leads are more viable opportunities to focus your selling efforts on.

Here are some tips for turning marketing leads into qualified sales leads:

- Offer a consultation call to learn about their specific needs

- Provide free trials or demos of your product/service

- Create content that nurtures leads based on where they are in the buyer's journey

- Use email sequences, chatbots, and live chat to qualify leads

- Identify when a lead exhibits key behaviors that indicate readiness to buy

- Incentivize leads to take the next step, like discounts for signing up for a demo

With a clear strategy to nurture marketing leads into sales-ready leads, you can maximize the value of your audience and improve conversion rates. Marketing generates leads, sales converts them. Work on building both!

From Leads to Profit: A Formula for Revenue Growth

In the business world, understanding the journey from leads to profit is crucial. This journey involves several key stages, each of which plays a vital role in determining your overall revenue and profit. Here's the straightforward formula for this journey:

Leads x Conversion Rate = Number of Transactions

This part of the formula represents the process of turning leads into actual transactions. Leads are potential customers who have shown interest in your product or service. The conversion rate is the percentage of these leads that convert into customers. For example, if you have 100 leads and 10 of them become customers, your conversion rate is 10%.

Improving either the number of leads or your conversion rate will result in a higher number of transactions. Therefore, strategies that increase lead generation or improve conversion rates (as discussed in the previous sections on visibility and conversion) are fundamental to revenue growth.

Number of Transactions x Transaction Value = Revenue

This step is about calculating your revenue. The total amount of money your business brings in is determined by multiplying the number of transactions (or sales) you make by the average value of each transaction.

For example, if you make 10 sales and each sale is worth $100, your revenue is $1,000. Increasing either the number of transactions or the value of each transaction will lead to a higher revenue. Therefore, strategies to promote repeat business, upselling, and cross-selling can be effective in this stage.

Revenue - Cost = Profit

Lastly, we arrive at the profit. This is the money you have left over after you subtract all of your costs from the revenue you've generated. Costs can include everything from production costs and overhead expenses to marketing and advertising costs.

For example, if your revenue is $1,000 and your total costs are $600, your profit is $400. Increasing revenue (as discussed in the previous steps) and managing costs effectively are the keys to maximizing profit.

In conclusion, the journey from leads to profit involves several key stages, each of which can be optimized to improve your overall financial performance. By understanding and using this formula, you can identify where to focus your efforts and how to strategically grow your revenue and profit.

If you want to fully outsource the lead generation, that's totally fine. However, if you want to multiply your revenue by 5, even 10 times, it's simple mathematics really - more leads open up more opportunities for you to clinch that sale!

And that's why we will go over 100 ways to get you leads. I'm really excited and I hope you are too.

Recap:

Let's recap some of the key points:

1. **Suspects are not Leads**: One of the most important distinctions we've made is that your Instagram followers, by default, are not leads. They start their journey as 'suspects'. These are individuals who have shown a basic level of interest in your brand by following your Instagram account. However, their engagement is often passive and does not go much beyond the occasional like or comment.

2. **Leads are Humans**: We've underscored the fact that behind each 'lead' is a real human being with unique interests, needs, and desires. Understanding this is critical to developing a successful marketing strategy. Instead of treating leads as mere data points or potential revenue sources, we need to engage with them on a human level, providing value and building meaningful connections.

3. **Growing Visibility to Grow Leads**: If the objective is to convert suspects into leads, then one of your primary goals should be to increase your brand visibility. This doesn't just mean increasing your follower count; it involves creating engaging, relevant, and valuable content that resonates

with your target audience. This way, you not only attract more people but also encourage deeper engagement, transitioning them from being 'suspects' to 'prospects', and eventually, to becoming leads.

Having established a firm understanding of what leads are and the importance of humanizing your systems in Chapter 1, we're now equipped to take the next significant step in our journey.

Chapter 2 is dedicated to building a robust lead generation system. This system won't just aid in increasing your brand's visibility, but it will also help create meaningful connections with your audience, transforming passive 'suspects' into engaged 'prospects', and eventually, loyal customers.

We'll delve into the **6 Elements of a Successful Client Attraction System**, all designed to guide your audience smoothly along the conversion path. So, let's turn the page and get started on creating a lead generation system that works for you.

Chapter 2

Building a Client Attraction System

A Journey from Networking Chaos to Lead Generation Mastery

Do you remember a time when you were brimming with excitement at networking events, collecting a heap of business cards, only to find yourself two years later drowning in cards and no real prospects? If you're nodding, trust me, you're not alone.

I once lived that paradox. I was a top producer, and I knew that sales and leads were inseparable. Yet, the barren desert of my prospects' list stared back at me. You might say I was lost in the vast galaxy of networking, rubbing elbows at the wrong places.

What's crazier is how I found my way out.

A Eureka Moment

I had a eureka moment: instead of attending events that gave me zero visibility, why not host my own? In my events, everyone got a piece of the spotlight. They spoke up; they were seen. This wasn't just an event where they handed out business cards and listened to monologues. Instead, it was a dynamic, interactive experience where real connections were forged. Participants were encouraged to share their stories, their dreams, and their business needs. It was a vibrant networking ecosystem, where each individual's voice was valued, creating a sense of community and collaboration. Gone were the days of aimless mingling; now, networking had purpose, direction, and most importantly, results.

That eureka moment was the genesis of a vibrant Austin community, but also the origin of my winning lead generation system.

If you've been networking, accumulating stacks of business cards, and yet finding no leads, it's not your fault. The reality is that few are teaching entrepreneurs how to navigate this vast ocean of connections. You've been told to go out and network, but then what? What are the specific steps to transform those business cards into meaningful relationships and eventually into leads? Or, even more pressing, how much time will you need to invest to make these connections fruitful? Without clear guidance, you may find yourself adrift, unsure of how to proceed.

By the way, if you're in Austin and want to expand your professional connections, please join our ATX PEN Group and be sure to follow our events calendar here.

In this chapter, we'll explore strategies to turn these questions into actionable insights.

You Don't Need To Add More Networking Events. You Need A System.

Yet, a nagging question lingered: **how do I speed up my networking activities so I could see more revenue without needing to attend more events?**

I needed a system - a machine - that could churn out leads even in my absence. This realization was my springboard into the world of automation and scalable systems.

And now, dear friend, I'm about to pull back the curtain on the 6 Key Components of a Successful Client Attraction System. These components will help you target customers from all angles, without pestering friends and family, and without devaluing your offer with crazy discounts.

6 Key Components of a Successful Client Attraction System

A successful client attraction system requires a thorough understanding of your desired customers, their concerns, how they recognize value, and what motivates them to utilize your services.

I can't emphasize enough the importance of having a client attraction system in place before diving headlong into lead generation. But don't misunderstand: I'm not talking about waiting for months before you start generating leads and closing sales. This process of creating your client attraction system can happen within hours. It's about being thoughtful and strategic, rather than rushing in without a plan.

So let's take this journey together and manifest your ideal client!

1. Defining Your Target Audience

Understanding and defining your target audience is the crucial starting point of an effective client attraction system. How can you tell if you have a defined audience? It's simple: you should be able to articulate it in one clear, concise sentence. This statement should encapsulate not only who your audience is but also what unique value you offer to them.

Here's an example of a well-defined audience: "I help construction businesses stand out online, so that they can grow." This sentence succinctly identifies the target audience (construction businesses) and outlines the specific problem being addressed (standing out online), followed by the ultimate goal or benefit (growth).

Does that mean that you don't help other markets? No. However, it means that you will focus your lead generation efforts in one market at a time. This targeted approach allows you to concentrate your resources where they are most effective, aligning your strategies with the specific needs and opportunities of each market segment.

2. Value Proposition

With your target audience clearly defined, the next step in building a successful lead generation system is crafting your value proposition. This is where you articulate how you will solve their main problem in a unique and valuable way.

Your value proposition is more than just a statement about what you do; it's a clear and compelling explanation of how you do it differently and better than anyone else. It outlines the specific benefits your target audience will receive and why they should choose you over your competitors.

Consider these key questions as you craft your value proposition:

- What is the primary problem or need that your target audience faces?

- How does your product or service uniquely address that problem or need?

- What specific benefits will your target audience gain by choosing your solution?

- Why should they trust you over your competitors?

Let's take our earlier example: "I help construction businesses stand out online, so that they can grow." The value proposition might expand on this by explaining the innovative digital marketing strategies used, the track record of success with similar businesses, and the personalized support and guidance provided throughout the process.

Your value proposition is the heart of your client attraction system. It communicates why you are the best choice for your target audience and compels them to engage with you. Crafting a powerful value proposition requires a deep understanding of your audience, a clear vision of your unique strengths, and the ability to convey that value in a way that resonates with your potential clients. It's the promise you make and the bridge that connects your target audience to the solutions they've been seeking.

Example 1: Digital Marketing Agency for Small Businesses

Value Proposition: "We transform construction businesses into local legends through tailored online marketing campaigns. Get more customers, build your brand, and grow faster with our specialized construction business focus."

Where Leads Can See It: Website homepage, social media profiles, email campaigns, Google Ads, and brochures distributed at local networking events.

Example 2: Eco-Friendly Cleaning Products Company

Value Proposition: "Clean your home and save the planet with our all-natural, biodegradable cleaning products. Enjoy a spotless home without harsh chemicals – good for you, good for the Earth."

Where Leads Can See It: Product packaging, website product pages, in-store displays, Facebook and Instagram ads, and informational leaflets at eco-friendly events.

Example 3: Personal Fitness Trainer Specializing in Senior Citizens

Value Proposition: "Rediscover strength, balance, and joy at any age with our personalized fitness programs designed for seniors. Feel young again with exercises tailored to your unique needs and abilities."

Where Leads Can See It: Personalized direct mail to retirement communities, website's "About Me" page, flyers at local community centers, LinkedIn profile, and introductory YouTube videos.

Example 4: AI-Powered Financial Planning App

Value Proposition: "Take control of your financial future with our AI-driven financial planning app. Receive personalized investment insights, track your goals, and build wealth effortlessly."

Where Leads Can See It: App store descriptions, website landing pages, sponsored posts on financial blogs, targeted Facebook and Twitter ads, and presentations at tech or finance conferences.

By strategically placing the value proposition in various locations where potential clients are likely to engage with your brand, you can effectively communicate the unique benefits of your product or service, thus attracting the right audience and converting them into loyal customers.

3. Touchpoints

Your client attraction system must incorporate multiple touchpoints, but why is this so vital? The reality is that leads rarely convert through a single marketing effort. In fact, studies have shown that it often takes an average of 6 to 8 touchpoints to generate a viable sales lead.

The presence of multiple touchpoints reflects the complexity of the customer journey, where potential clients interact with your brand in various ways before making a decision. By providing consistent and relevant engagement across different platforms, you enhance your visibility and credibility, thereby fostering a stronger connection with your target audience.

This multi-touch approach ensures that you're meeting potential clients where they are, whether it's through social media, email marketing, in-person events, or other channels. By nurturing leads through a well-thought-out sequence of touchpoints, you increase the likelihood of conversion, building a more robust and resilient client attraction system.

Consider this: a nurtured lead makes a purchase that is 47% larger than a non-nurtured lead. In a world where customers are bombarded with marketing messages, personalized and consistent engagement across multiple touchpoints not only helps you stand out but also builds trust, ensuring that your leads feel seen and understood.

Here are examples of multiple touchpoints that can be part of a client attraction system:

Website: Your main hub where potential clients can find detailed information about your services, read testimonials, and access valuable content like blogs or ebooks.

Social Media Channels: Platforms like Facebook, Twitter, LinkedIn, and Instagram allow you to engage with your audience through regular posts, videos, stories, and direct messaging.

Email Marketing: Regular newsletters, promotional emails, and personalized follow-ups can keep potential clients engaged and informed about your latest offers and news.

In-person Events: Hosting or attending workshops, seminars, networking events, or trade shows provides an opportunity to engage with potential clients face-to-face.

Webinars and Online Workshops: Offering free or paid online educational content can showcase your expertise and provide value to potential clients.

Customer Support: Providing excellent customer service through live chat, phone support, or FAQs can build trust and foster a positive relationship with potential clients.

Content Marketing: Sharing valuable and informative content through blogs, ebooks, whitepapers, or podcasts can establish your authority in the field and draw potential clients closer to your brand.

Retargeting Ads: Utilizing online advertising that targets users who have already shown interest in your products or services can keep your brand at the top of their minds.

Loyalty Programs: Offering rewards or incentives for repeat engagements or referrals can build a lasting relationship with existing clients and attract new ones.

Direct Mail: Even in a digital age, personalized postcards, letters, or brochures can still be an effective way to reach potential clients.

Interactive Tools and Quizzes: Providing interactive tools or quizzes related to your services on your website can engage visitors and provide personalized recommendations.

Community Engagement: Participating in community events or online forums related to your industry can enhance your brand's reputation and allow you to connect with potential clients.

Video Marketing: Creating engaging videos on platforms like YouTube or embedding them on your site can visually showcase your products or services.

Referral Programs: Encouraging satisfied customers to refer others to your business can create a trustworthy and organic lead generation channel.

These various touchpoints create a holistic engagement strategy, providing multiple opportunities to connect with your target audience, understand their needs, and guide them towards your offerings.

Pro Tip: Don't make it complicated for your lead to find you. Whether it's through clear and concise website navigation, easily accessible contact information, user-friendly social media profiles, or straightforward calls to action, always strive to provide a seamless and intuitive experience. The less effort it takes for a potential client to understand what you offer and how to engage with you, the more likely they are to take that next step. Simplicity often trumps complexity in creating a customer-friendly experience. Make yourself available and approachable across all platforms and watch how your leads convert into loyal clients.

Attract more clients with a funnel

A funnel, in marketing terms, refers to the journey a potential customer takes through a series of steps, leading them from initial awareness of a product or service to the final goal of conversion into a customer. This process is often depicted in a funnel shape, showing many prospects at the top, narrowing down to the few who become customers.

Now, let's develop a strategy for a funnel using the example of a cleaning company:

1. Awareness (Top of the Funnel):

- Social Media Advertising: Share engaging content about cleaning tips and hacks, promoting the company's values and mission, possibly offering a free cleaning guide.

- Content Marketing: Regular blog posts that provide valuable information on maintaining a clean and healthy environment, showcasing the expertise of the cleaning company.

2. **Interest (Upper Mid-Funnel):**

   - Email Marketing Campaigns: A targeted series of emails providing more insights into the cleaning services, special offers, and inviting them to sign up for a newsletter.

   - SEO: An optimized website that ranks high in search results for cleaning services in the relevant geographic location, allowing potential customers to easily find the company.

3. **Consideration (Lower Mid-Funnel):**

   - Webinars and Live Demonstrations: Hosting live webinars to demonstrate cleaning techniques, tools used, and the exceptional standards maintained by the cleaning staff.

   - Referral Programs: Encouraging satisfied customers to refer friends and family, possibly through discounts or special offers.

4. **Intent (Bottom of the Funnel):**

   - Retargeting Campaigns: Ads targeted at those who have shown interest in the services but have not yet converted, perhaps offering a special first-time customer discount.

- Physical Locations (if applicable): For local cleaning services, in-store promotions or community engagement events to meet potential clients in person and build trust.

5. Purchase (Conversion):

- Website Landing Pages: Creating compelling landing pages with a clear call-to-action, such as booking a cleaning appointment or a free consultation.

- Personalization: Offering tailored cleaning packages, understanding customer needs and preferences, and providing personalized quotes.

6. Retention (Post-Conversion):

- Customer Service and Follow-up Emails: Ensuring customer satisfaction through excellent service and follow-up communication, asking for feedback, and offering incentives for repeat business.

7. Advocacy:

- Loyalty Programs and Social Proof: Encouraging satisfied customers to become advocates for the brand, through testimonials, reviews, and possibly a loyalty program that offers ongoing discounts or rewards.

This funnel for a cleaning company moves prospects from the initial awareness stage through various touchpoints that nurture their interest and intent, ultimately converting them into customers, and further into advocates for the brand. It offers a systematic approach to lead generation and customer acquisition, guiding potential clients through a thoughtfully crafted pathway tailored to the cleaning industry.

Reminder: A funnel doesn't need to be complex to be effective. Here's a simple, streamlined version for a cleaning company:

1. Social Media Post: A single engaging post about a special cleaning offer, with a link to a landing page.

2. Landing Page: A simple landing page on the website with details about the offer, cleaning services provided, and a form to sign up for more information.

3. Email Follow-up: A personalized email sent to those who signed up, providing more information about the

cleaning services and inviting them to schedule a cleaning appointment.

4. Booking Page: A user-friendly page where customers can easily book a cleaning appointment, choose the services they need, and see the pricing.

5. Thank You Email: A thank-you email after the service is completed, asking for feedback and offering a discount for future bookings.

This basic funnel allows the cleaning company to generate awareness, capture interest, and guide potential clients to conversion with minimal touchpoints. It's easy to set up and can be an effective way to attract and retain customers without overwhelming them with too many options or steps. Sometimes, simplicity is key to connecting with your audience and achieving your marketing goals.

4. Irresistible Offer

We've covered landing pages as a touchpoint in your client attraction system. If you've already used landing pages and they didn't generate enough leads, chances are, they lacked an irresistible offer. But what makes an offer irresistible? The answer lies in the WOW effect.

An irresistible offer is all about creating that "WOW effect" that makes it almost impossible for potential clients to pass up. It's the captivating element that grabs their attention and compels them to take immediate action.

Crafting the Irresistible Offer

To craft such an offer, you'll need to consider several essential components:

1. Understand Your Audience's Pain Points: Start by knowing exactly what problem your target audience is facing that your product or service can solve. This deep understanding enables you to tailor your offer directly to their most pressing needs, making it highly relevant and attractive.

2. Provide Exceptional Value: An irresistible offer must go beyond the standard offering. Include something extra that sets it apart. It could be a significant discount, a free add-on service, exclusive access to something, or any additional benefit that adds tangible value.

3. Create a Sense of Urgency: Introducing elements of scarcity, such as limited time offers, limited quantities, or exclusive access for a specific duration, can create a sense of urgency. This scarcity makes the offer feel even more appealing.

4. Make It Clear and Simple: Ensure that the prospects know exactly what they're getting and why it's a fantastic deal. Clarity is key to making an offer truly irresistible.

5. Provide Social Proof: Incorporate testimonials or endorsements that demonstrate the value of your offer. Knowing that others have benefited from what you're offering can be a highly persuasive element.

Example for a Cleaning Company:

"Get our premium home cleaning package at 30% off, plus a free deep cleaning of one room of your choice! Offer valid only for the first 50 bookings this month."

In this example, the cleaning company is not only offering a substantial discount but also adding a complimentary service (deep cleaning of one room) and creating urgency with a limited number of bookings. This combination transforms a regular promotion into something genuinely irresistible, compelling more prospects to engage with the service.

5. Personalization

In today's highly competitive market, businesses that want to stand out need to show customers that they understand and care about their unique preferences and needs.

Nobody wants to feel that they're getting the same deal that everyone gets. Statistics show that personalization can significantly enhance customer engagement and conversion rates. According to a report by Epsilon, 80% of consumers are more likely to do business with a company that offers personalized experiences. Moreover, a study by Accenture has revealed that 91% of consumers are more likely to shop with brands that recognize, remember, and provide relevant offers and recommendations.

Personalization isn't just about inserting the person's name in your massive email.

What is Personalization?

Personalization is the process of creating customized experiences for individuals. It means that instead of sending the same email, offering the same discount, or using the same sales pitch for everyone, you're adapting these elements to resonate with the particular person you're engaging.

How to Implement Personalization

Here's how you can integrate personalization into your client attraction system:

1. Gather Data: Collect information about your customers through surveys, interactions, purchase history, and other methods. Understand what they like, what they need, and how they engage with your business.

2. Segment Your Audience: Break down your audience into smaller groups based on specific characteristics, such as demographics, purchasing behavior, or preferences. This segmentation allows for more targeted communication.

3. Tailor Your Messaging: Use the information you've gathered to create tailored messages. Whether it's an email, advertisement, or a product recommendation, ensure that it speaks directly to the person's unique needs and interests.

4. Offer Customized Products or Services: If possible, offer options that allow the customer to personalize their purchase. This could be as simple as allowing them to choose a color, a package, or including an extra feature that they find valuable.

5. Monitor and Adjust: Continuously analyze how your personalized efforts are performing. Adjust as needed to ensure that you're meeting your customers' expectations and maximizing your results.

Example for a Cleaning Company:

"Dear [Customer's Name], we noticed that you often book our kitchen cleaning service. As a token of our appreciation, we're offering you a 20% discount on your next kitchen cleaning, plus a complimentary cleaning of your oven."

Pro Tip: Lead Scoring

A crucial part of personalization is understanding which leads have the most potential to convert into customers. Implementing a lead scoring system within your CRM allows you to rank contacts based on their likelihood to engage with your business. By assigning a high score to promising leads, you can channel them to your business developer, who can then nurture those connections using targeted social media interactions.

This method helps you maximize your resources and ensures that your marketing efforts are focused on the areas where they're most likely to produce results.

6. Lead Nurturing

Think of your customer attraction system as a well-oiled engine. Every part must be in sync for the engine to perform at its peak, and lead nurturing is an essential component that cannot be overlooked.

While traditional lead follow-up strategies focus on immediate conversion, attraction marketing requires a different approach. It's not just about chasing a sale; it's about building relationships and trust. Your goal is to demonstrate that you understand your prospects' needs and that you have the solution they seek.

Here's how to effectively nurture leads within your client attraction system:

1. **Provide Value First**: Share content and insights that address the pain points of your prospects. Offering valuable information helps position you as an expert in your field.

2. **Engage in Meaningful Conversations**: Rather than pushing a sales agenda, engage with your leads in genuine dialogue. Ask questions, provide thoughtful answers, and show that you're interested in their concerns.

3. **Utilize Multi-Channel Outreach**: Reach your leads where they are, whether that's through email, social media, or a phone call. Different leads may respond to different channels, so it's wise to use a combination.

4. **Personalize Your Communication**: Tailor your messages based on the information you have about the lead. Personalization increases the chances of engagement, making the prospect feel seen and understood.

5. **Maintain Consistent Contact**: Lead nurturing is a gradual process. Regular, non-intrusive follow-up demonstrates your continued interest and keeps you on the prospect's radar without being pushy.

6. **Analyze and Adjust**: Keep track of your interactions and analyze what works and what doesn't. Make necessary adjustments to ensure that your lead nurturing strategies align with the needs and interests of your target audience.

Remember, lead nurturing within a client attraction system is about more than immediate results. It's a sustained effort to build credibility, foster relationships, and, ultimately, guide prospects through the funnel until they are ready to become your clients. Patience, empathy, and a strategic approach are key to nurturing leads effectively and converting them into loyal customers.

Here's a recap of the 6 key elements of a client attraction system:

1. Defining Your Target Audience: Understanding and identifying the specific market or group you aim to reach. This involves recognizing their needs, preferences, and pain points.

2. Value Proposition: Determining how you will address and solve the main problem of your target audience in a unique and valuable way. Your value proposition should communicate why you are the best choice for them.

3. Touchpoints (Funnel Strategy): Designing multiple points of interaction with your potential clients, from initial awareness to conversion. This often includes a planned sequence of interactions, such as emails, social media engagement, and landing pages.

4. Irresistible Offer: Crafting an offer that stands out and compels your target audience to engage. It must have the "WOW" effect that makes it difficult for potential clients to refuse.

5. Personalization: Tailoring your outreach and offers to suit individual preferences and needs. Personalization helps

you connect on a deeper level and makes potential clients feel special and understood.

6. Lead Nurturing: Implementing strategies to build long-term relationships with potential clients. Lead nurturing involves a sustained effort to provide value, engage in meaningful conversations, and guide prospects through the sales funnel until they are ready to buy.

By strategically combining these six elements, you can create a client attraction system that not only generates leads but also builds strong relationships and converts those leads into loyal customers. It's a holistic approach that goes beyond traditional sales tactics to foster trust, demonstrate value, and drive growth.

Chapter 3
100 Ways to Generate Leads

All that talk about concepts and terms? When does the actual lead generation start? Now. In this chapter, we will explore 100 ways to generate leads using various methods and channels. Every method and channel we've picked is unique in its regard.

I've segmented the generation leads into their categories for ease. Make sure to go through each of them step by step to add them to your digital marketing strategies accordingly. We will also be walking through guerilla tactics that will kick-start your lead generation almost immediately.

Social Media (1-20)

1. Use relevant hashtags like #smallbusiness on posts to reach more people.

2. Analyze posts with free analytics tools to optimize content.

3. Create fun TikTok and Instagram Reels showcasing your business, like a bakery making cakes.

4. Run contests on Instagram for free products/services.

5. Partner with nano influencers in your industry to promote your brand.

6. Use location tags and stickers in social media posts to increase local visibility.

7. Promote discounts and deals for followers on social media.

8. Share user-generated content that mentions your business.

9. Go live on Facebook or Instagram to engage your followers.

10. Use clicks-to-call ads on Facebook to get leads calling your business.

11. Partner with businesses in complementary industries to co-host a LinkedIn Live discussion.

12. Ask followers questions to spark conversation and feedback.

13. Join Facebook Groups in your niche and provide value by answering questions.

14. Send personalized connection requests on LinkedIn with a custom message.

15. Join a social media contest hosted by another brand.

16. Host a virtual event like a webinar focused on topics your audience cares about.

17. Launch targeted ads promoting content upgrades like a checklist or template.

18. Send direct messages on social media answering prospect questions or providing helpful tips.

19. Promote your Instagram profile via a website link or email signature.

20. Tag industry leaders when you mention or reference them in social posts.

Content Marketing (21-40)

1. Interview experts for your blog in your industry.

2. Create "How To" tutorials relevant to your business.

3. Develop case studies demonstrating solutions for clients.

4. Send helpful follow-up emails when people sign up on your website.

5. Give away free educational tools like calculators, templates, or ebooks in exchange for opt-ins.

6. Write comprehensive guides and checklists related to your product or service.

7. Share statistics and research about your industry.

8. Create and share infographics visualizing data or ideas related to your business.

9. Write reviews of products or services your target customers use.

10. Answer common customer questions in blog posts or FAQ pages.

11. Guest post on other blogs in your industry with useful content.

12. Curate and share lists of the best resources related to your niche.

13. Promote your most popular and high-quality content periodically.

14. Repurpose content into multiple formats like text, audio, video.

15. Offer a free course via email designed to educate prospects.

16. Interview customers about their experience with your business.

17. Send personalized emails when website visitors browse specific pages.

18. Create comparison articles contrasting products/services in your niche.

19. Leverage online press release distribution to announce new products, services, achievements.

20. Syndicate your blog content across other platforms.

Guerilla Marketing (41-50)

1. Partner with local businesses to distribute flyers or coupons.

2. Sponsor a little league team and attend games.

3. Set up demonstrations or activities related to your business in public areas.

4. Stick branded magnets or bumper stickers on cars with permission.

5. Use sidewalk chalk art or stencils with your brand name near relevant events.

6. Rent ad space on notice boards or benches at high-traffic locations.

7. Provide free product samples at local events you sponsor or attend.

8. Partner with complementary businesses to reach each other's customers.

9. Cold approach potential customers in your area with personalized offers.

10. Set up a booth at busy community hubs to engage residents.

Demand Generation Campaigns (51-75)

1. Run Google Search ads with discounts for landing page visitors.

2. Advertise on niche membership sites related to your target customers.

3. Sponsor or exhibit at industry conferences your prospects attend.

4. Reach out offering free product trials or demos for targeted prospects.

5. Run retargeting ads across the web for website visitors.

6. Create "squeeze" landing pages to capture leads in exchange for an offer.

7. Develop a free tool or calculator relevant to your audience.

8. Send direct mail campaigns with promotions or personalized offers to targeted buyer lists.

9. Partner with complementary businesses to co-create content and co-host webinars.

10. Enter to win an award and motivate your audience with a contest so they can vote for you.

11. Launch a limited-time flash sale or special promotion across marketing channels.

12. Buy paid product placement in relevant digital publications.

13. Attend in-person networking events to connect with prospects.

14. Set up email or website pop-up offers when visitors are browsing or exiting your site.

15. Collaborate with influencers and creators to develop sponsored content about your brand.

16. Sponsor podcast ads on shows relevant to your target audience.

17. Promote discounts for customers who refer friends or colleagues.

18. Send direct mail gifts or packages to selected high-value prospects.

19. Create an ebook, checklist or tool related to your product and promote it across platforms.

20. Write and distribute press releases announcing company news and achievements.

21. Develop and promote educational blog content around customer pain points.

22. Sponsor local events that your target customers attend like races, fairs, concerts.

23. Raffle a high ticket item.

24. Partner with industry suppliers to co-develop content and cross-promote.

25. Conduct and promote polls, surveys and questionnaires for current/potential customers.

Co-Marketing (76-85)

1. Co-host a webinar with an industry expert to cross-promote.

2. Create co-branded content and assets with a strategic partner.

3. Develop joint packages or bundled offers together with a complementary business.

4. Swap endorsements, testimonials, and backlinks with relevant brands.

5. Co-sponsor a local team or community event with a partner business.

6. Promote partners' offers and content to your current customer base.

7. Participate together in local business expos and events with a partner vendor.

8. Share costs of advertising and marketing campaigns with aligned businesses.

9. Co-produce a campaign together with a strategic partner.

10. Offer discounts or incentives to each other's customer bases as part of a co-marketing agreement.

Leveraging Platforms (86-100)

1. Create a profile on LinkedIn to connect with professionals.

2. Develop courses on online education platforms like Udemy.

3. Answer industry questions on Quora to demonstrate expertise.

4. Join and participate in relevant online forums and communities.

5. Promote your podcast across various platforms like Spotify and Apple.

6. List your services on freelancing sites like Upwork.

7. Develop a presence on industry websites and niche networks.

8. Promote your brand across your website, social media, email signatures, etc.

9. Build partnerships with vendors in your industry value chain.

10. Launch custom branded merchandise for fans and customers.

11. Attend virtual conferences and events in your niche.

12. Distribute press releases on platforms like PRWeb.

13. Syndicate your blog content on sites like Medium.

14. Join and contribute to industry publications and online magazines.

15. Utilize SEO consistently to improve search visibility and traffic.

Implementing even a handful of these tactics can generate more quality leads for your business in any industry. Let me know if you would like me to elaborate on any particular strategy or provide more examples. The key is to test different approaches and see what resonates best with your target audience. With some dedication and experimentation, you can build an effective lead generation program leveraging the power of digital marketing and content.

I hope these 100 lead generation ideas have sparked some inspiration for your business! While it may seem overwhelming, you don't need to implement all of these tactics at once.

Start small and focus on selecting just 5-10 strategies that seem the most relevant for your business and target audience. Try a mix of short-term lead generation channels like social media and paid ads along with longer-term content marketing plays.

Give each new tactic enough time and iteration to determine if it is moving the needle before diversifying too much. As you find approaches that work, you can optimize and scale those while layering in new experiments.

Be sure to track your results so you know which strategies are generating the most quality leads and ROI. Not every approach will be a winner, and that's okay. Lead generation is an ongoing process of testing and learning in your unique market.

The most important thing is to not get overwhelmed. Have fun brainstorming new ideas and getting creative with your marketing. Focus on providing genuine value, building relationships and becoming a trusted resource for your ideal customers.

With a strategic, customer-focused approach, these tactics can help take your lead generation to the next level. But don't try to do it all at once! Start small, track results and double down on what works. Wishing you the best as you grow your business and customer base.

While this chapter covered 100 great lead generation tactics, I have an even more powerful book coming soon that will take your results to the next level.

Introducing our upcoming book: 88 To Greatness. This will reveal the proven formula to go from zero to hero in just 88 days, step-by-step.

Inside 88 To Greatness, you'll discover:

- The 10x Lead Generation Method to get a flood of qualified prospects in your pipeline

- The 7 Core Funnels for transforming curious visitors into loyal, high-lifetime-value customers

- The DAILY ACTION PLAN to follow over 12 weeks to compound your growth

- And much more!

Be sure to follow my Instagram @jessicacamposofficial and @marketingforgreatness and visit www.88togreatness.com to get on the early-access list.

This is the fastest way to implement everything we covered today and achieve explosive business growth in 88 days or less. Don't miss it!

I can't wait to get this book into your hands and help you rapidly grow using the exclusive 10x Lead Gen Formula. Get ready for your best year in business yet!

Chapter 4

Overcoming Lead Generation Roadblocks

Generating a steady flow of leads is crucial for business growth. But many business owners struggle to gain traction. In this chapter, we'll diagnose the most common reasons your lead generation efforts may be failing - and how to fix them.

Lack of Visibility

If potential customers can't find you, they can't buy from you. Improving your visibility needs to be priority one.

- Leverage SEO to boost your search rankings. Research keywords, optimize pages, and build backlinks.

- Run paid ads on platforms like Facebook and Google to increase awareness. Target your ideal demographics.

- Create engaging content on social media and interact regularly to expand your audience.

- Network online and in-person at industry events to connect with prospects.

- Consider guest posting on authority sites related to your niche to tap into new audiences.

Unclear Marketing Messaging

Does your messaging clearly explain who you serve and the value you provide? Confused prospects may disengage.

- Define your ideal customer avatar (ICA) so you can tailor content accordingly.

- Refine your value proposition - why should the ICA buy from you? What pain points do you solve?

- Audit your website/ads to ensure consistent messaging optimized for your ICA.

- Create and prominently display content addressing common buyer questions.

- Use testimonials and case studies to showcase concrete examples of the value you provide.

No Structured Lead Nurturing System

Attracting leads is only the first step. You need to systematically nurture them toward conversion.

- Build an email sequence to engage prospects - like a 5-part "Getting Started" series.

- Offer lead magnets in exchange for contact info - ebooks, tip sheets, guides related to their interests.

- Add value on social media by answering prospects' questions publicly.

- Use chatbots or live chat to qualify leads and address concerns in real-time.

- Retarget cold leads with personalized content recommendations based on their engagement.

The Bottom Line

Follow this advice to get visibility, clarify your marketing, and implement structured lead nurturing. Don't get discouraged if it takes testing and optimization to get it right. Consistency and high-value content tailored to your ICA are key.

Chapter 5

Unlocking Growth with Forensic Marketing

In previous chapters, we covered strategies for generating more leads. But attracting leads is only step one. You also need to understand why prospects convert into customers - or don't. That's where forensic marketing comes in.

What is Forensic Marketing?

Forensic marketing involves gathering data and analyzing metrics to identify opportunities and bottlenecks in your sales and marketing funnel. It takes a research-based approach to diagnosing issues so you can optimize conversion rates.

Benefits of Forensic Marketing:

- Pinpoint exactly where leads are dropping out of your funnel
- Understand why prospects choose not to convert
- Identify strengths and weaknesses in your sales process

- Improve messaging and positioning for better resonance

- Develop targeted solutions to fix conversion barriers

Conducting a forensic marketing analysis provides data-driven insights you can act on to close more leads.

Key Forensic Marketing Tools

Here are some essential tools to enable an effective forensic marketing approach:

- Google Analytics - Track website visitor behavior and conversion metrics.

- Marketing automation software - Score and route leads based on interactions. We recommend Kartra. Grab a free trial offer on us!

- Email tracking - See email open and click-through rates.

- Form analytics - Identify which form fields have high abandon rates.

- Live chat transcripts - Uncover questions and objections.

- Feedback surveys - Ask for prospects for direct input on why they didn't convert.

By leveraging these technologies, you can gather crucial data on the customer journey and pinpoint how to improve conversions.

The Takeaway

Forensic marketing represents a shift from guesswork to evidence-based decision making. Analyzing metrics, interactions, and feedback across touchpoints paints a clear picture of where you are losing leads and why. Implementing the right tools provides the visibility needed to course-correct and turn more prospects into satisfied customers.

Chapter 6

AI Marketing - The Cutting Edge of Lead Generation

Artificial intelligence (AI) has transformed marketing much like it has revolutionized everything else. In this comprehensive chapter, we will explore how AI-driven marketing can take your lead generation to the next level.

And, of course, we need to talk about AI □

What is AI Marketing?

AI marketing refers to leveraging artificial intelligence technologies to automate, analyze, personalize, and optimize marketing campaigns and processes. Key techniques include:

- Machine learning - Systems that can learn from data without explicit programming

- Natural language processing - Understanding and generating human language

- Predictive analytics - Identifying patterns to forecast future outcomes

- **Chatbots** - Automated messaging programs that engage prospects

Benefits of AI Marketing

Implementing AI delivers a myriad of advantages:

- **More Relevant Content** - AI can analyze buyer personas and previous engagement to recommend content that resonates better with each lead.

- **Improved Segmentation** - Machine learning algorithms can segment audiences and define micro-targeting strategies more accurately.

- **Faster Optimization** - AI tools test variations of marketing elements like subject lines to optimize performance.

- **Higher Conversions** - Chatbots engage every lead 24/7, answering questions and converting at scale.

- **Lower Costs** - Automation reduces manual tasks, allowing teams to focus on higher value activities.

- **Better Experiences** - AI delivers personalized experiences, predictive recommendations, and relevant conversations.

With these capabilities, AI augments human marketers to drive better results.

The 50-50 AI Marketing Framework

We've been using AI tools for about 2 years now. And here's our take: when leveraging AI for marketing, the most effective approach is a 50-50 blend of human expertise and AI capabilities.

Here is an overview of this balanced framework:

The Human Role:

- Set overall strategy and objectives

- Identify focus areas for AI implementation

- Structure datasets, taxonomies, and metrics

- Steer AI tools and adjust parameters

- Interpret insights and make recommendations

- Manage cross-channel coordination and budgets

- Oversee campaign creative and messaging

- Continuously find areas for optimization

The AI Role:

- Process massive amounts of data for insights
- Test content variations and personalized messaging at scale
- Optimize and automate campaign execution
- Monitor channels and user behavior in real-time
- Model outcomes to predict future results
- Route leads and recommend next-best actions
- Rapidly produce content variations for testing
- Execute repetitive tasks like reporting and analysis

With humans providing the vision and guidance while AI handles high-volume execution and iteration, marketing programs can scale and optimize at unprecedented speeds. AI removes bottlenecks while humans direct its capabilities for maximum business impact.

This 50-50 balance of strategy with automation, creativity with analysis, and oversight with augmentation covers all the bases to get the most out of AI-driven marketing. This is how we've been able to help our clients grow quicker.

Best Uses of AI Marketing for Business Owners

AI for Smarter Content Creation

Producing high-quality content that resonates with your audience is essential for lead generation but often difficult to scale manually. AI writing assistants leverage natural language processing to transform content creation.

Benefits include:

- Generating blog posts and articles from keywords and topics

- Producing multiple variations of content for A/B testing

- Optimizing writing for specific target personas or scenarios

- Creating landing pages, email sequences, ad copy, and more

- Augmenting human writing with personalized insights

For example, tools like Content At Scale can craft entire blog posts from a title that are ready to publish or refine further. This allows rapid content ideation and production.

Bringing AI to Your Business Without Overwhelm

In working with many business owners on lead generation, I've found most are aware of AI marketing but feel overwhelmed about actually implementing it.

That's why my team and I have developed an approach to bring the power of AI to your business in a simple, stress-free way:

- We've built an AI content marketing dashboard where our clients can easily view and manage AI-generated content. You'll get a firsthand look at how our bots create draft blog posts, social media posts, emails and more based on your goals.

- With our 50-50 method, professional human writers then refine this AI content to ensure it is high-quality and 100% authentic to your brand voice.

- Our SEO experts additionally optimize the content so it ranks well and drives traffic.

What you get is a streamlined, transparent AI content production system bolstered by human oversight. You don't need technical expertise to benefit from it.

We handle all the heavy lifting to identify the best AI tools, integrate them into proven processes, produce relevant content at scale, and optimize results.

You simply provide our dashboard with your strategy, topics and approval, while we activate personalized AI content marketing for your business.

This takes the complexity out and makes it easy to reap the rewards of AI. Our clients love having more original, engaging content consistently without the headaches.

Here are some examples of ideal use cases for our AI content marketing solution:

- SEO Content
  Our AI can churn out legions of optimized blog posts, articles, and web copy tailored to target keywords. This massively boosts website content for organic search rankings.

- Local SEO
  The AI can generate location-optimized content for cities/regions you serve to improve local search visibility.

- **Social Media**
  Let the AI create a high-volume of posts, captions, and snippets across all your social profiles to engage followers.

- **Guides & Ebooks**
  Produce guides, ebooks, whitepapers, and lead magnets at scale by simply providing topics and outlines to the AI.

- **Workshop Creation**
  Our AI can transcribe workshop/webinar recordings and automatically create written summaries, takeaways, and blog posts recapping the content.

The natural language capabilities make it possible to quickly craft unlimited amounts of original, high-quality content personalized to your brand across every digital channel and format.

Whether you need content for your website, social media, lead generation offers, local targeting, or thought leadership, our AI solution has you covered. Let us know which use cases are most relevant for your business and we'll ensure the AI is customized for your specific needs. Book a demo today!

The Future of AI Marketing

AI marketing will become table stakes as adoption grows. Here are some predictions:

- Chatbots and messaging will become the dominant customer touchpoints

- Content will be dynamically customized based on individual profiles

- Ads and emails will respond in real-time based on behavior

- Recommendation engines will know exactly what each person wants

- Optimization will be continuous and hands-free

- Buying journeys will become radically personalized

Businesses who embrace AI now will have a decisive advantage in reaching and engaging customers amidst this transformation.

Over to You

AI marketing presents game-changing opportunities to attract and convert more leads. With the right strategy, AI can become your digital marketing powerhouse executing tasks better and faster than ever before. What AI marketing applications are you most excited about leveraging? How do you plan to implement this powerful technology for your business? The possibilities are endless.

BONUS Chapter
The Mindset for Rapid Business Growth

Introduction: A Personal Success Story

About two years ago, my business partner and I embarked on a thrilling and uncertain journey. We started our MFG-SEO agency with just under $10,000 in our account. That's not a significant sum when launching a business, but we were driven by a vision and the belief that we could create something remarkable.

We decided to pour everything we had into that vision, guided not only by a strategic plan but also a mindset focused on growth, perseverance, and adaptability. Fast forward to two years later, we had grown our business to a $1M valuation and found a strategic partner.

How did it happen?

It wasn't just about implementing the concrete methods I've shared throughout this book. While those strategies were instrumental, they wouldn't have been as effective without the right MINDSET.

Here's how we approached growth, and how you can apply the same principles to your business:

1. Think Big Picture: From day one, we kept our long-term vision front and center. It informed our daily decisions and kept us aligned with where we wanted to go. By focusing on the big picture, you can ensure that short-term challenges don't derail your progress.

2. Be Obsessed with Speed: We understood that in the competitive world of business, speed was everything. We structured our days for maximum productivity and agility, allowing us to respond quickly to opportunities and challenges.

3. Value Consistency Over Intensity: Rather than engaging in sporadic intense efforts that lead to burnout, we focused on making consistent daily progress. This compound effect helped us achieve more than we could have through inconsistent bursts of effort.

4. Embrace Discomfort: Growth requires pushing past comfort zones. We regularly sought new challenges and opportunities that forced us to grow and adapt. Embrace discomfort, and you'll find new levels of success.

5. Fall in Love with Systems: Efficiency was key to our growth. We designed systems that could run smoothly even without our constant intervention. By streamlining processes, you can focus more on growth and less on maintenance.

6. Measure Everything: Data was our guiding star. We tracked key metrics obsessively, providing clarity and insight into our performance. Measure everything, and you'll never be in the dark about your business's health.

7. Keep Eyes on the Horizon: Staying abreast of industry trends helped us adapt and innovate. Never get complacent. Always look ahead and be ready to evolve.

8. Become Obsessed with Customers: Our customers were our North Star. By putting their needs first and solving for them, we built a loyal and growing client base.

9. Maintain Positive Energy: Energy and attitude were as vital as strategy. We cultivated daily habits that kept our spirits high and our minds focused.

10. Outwork Everyone: There were no shortcuts in our journey. We understood that consistent extra hours would compound over time, leading us to our goals.

Yes, we faced obstacles, but by sticking to these principles, no challenge was insurmountable. This mindset, combined with the methods detailed in this book, can be your roadmap to rapid business growth.

The journey may not be easy, but with the right mindset, it can be incredibly rewarding. Adopt these principles, and you'll be well on your way to achieving your business goals faster than you ever imagined possible. Whether you're starting with $10,000 or $10, the mindset for rapid growth is within your grasp. Embrace it, and watch your business soar.

This exclusive content is an excerpt from the upcoming book - 88 To Greatness: Going from Zero to Hero in 88 Days. Sign up here to get access to the book as soon as it's out!

About Jessica Campos, Founder of Marketing for Greatness

Jessica Campos is the passionate and driven founder of Marketing for Greatness, a company dedicated to helping small businesses and entrepreneurs excel in the ever-changing world of marketing and lead generation. With years of experience in the industry, Jessica has honed her skills in various aspects of marketing, including social media, content creation, and SEO.

Throughout her career, Jessica has led multi-million dollar marketing campaigns for popular brands such as Beachbody and Spectrum. Her expertise has been recognized by industry-leading platforms like Social Media Examiner, where she has educated professionals on effective marketing strategies and tactics.

Jessica is an attorney-turned-marketer. As her law career progressed, she found it very challenging to mix her career with her never-ending tasks as a new mom. The idea of building a business that could be worked from anywhere was exciting. So she decided to build an online business using affiliate marketing. And a few years later, she canceled her attorney license to fully dedicate herself to pursuing 2 passions: helping businesses and growing a family. She is a mom of 4, a well-known leader in Austin, and a friend to many.

Jessica's mission is to empower businesses to build strong client attraction systems that generate leads consistently and effectively. She believes in building genuine relationships, gaining brand authority, and standing out from the competition. Her hands-on approach and commitment to her client's success have earned her a reputation as a trusted expert.

In addition to her work at Marketing for Greatness, Jessica is a sought-after speaker, sharing her knowledge and expertise at conferences and events worldwide. She is also a published author, contributing articles to various industry platforms and sharing her insights with a wider audience.

Jessica's dedication to helping small businesses and entrepreneurs succeed is what sets her apart from the rest. Through Marketing for Greatness, she provides the tools, strategies, and support necessary for businesses to thrive in today's competitive market. Her unwavering commitment to her client's success is what makes her a true leader in the world of marketing and lead generation.

Made in the USA
Monee, IL
23 September 2023